JORDA

RELATIONSHIP
seasons

ASSETS,
LIABILITIES,
AND LESSONS
LEARNED

Table of Contents

By the end of this read you should be able to distinguish the difference in your everyday relationships. You should be able to categorize the positive relationships and gravitate towards them. You Should also be able to identify if any relationships are missing in your life. You are in control of your future. You are in control of your relationships. Make them count and make them the best they can be.

"Never underestimate the power of Good Relationships"

By: Jordan M Shade

Are you struggling to try to determine where you stand in a relationship or possibly where the other person stands in the relationship? Do you sometimes find yourself seeking confirmation of the relationship's worth? Question no more. Young or old, rich, or poor, I've written this book to help you answer some of the many questions you have floating around in your head.

Such as Liability relationships: aren't all bad some of them are lessons. But they won't turn into that until you let them go. Let go of the liability relationships so you can see the lesson in them!

I hope you will enjoy reading this book as much as I enjoyed writing it. May God Bless you and Keep you

www.JordanShade.com

Dedication

This book is dedicated to my Grandparents, Pastor George and Marjorie Shade who have been married for 55 years and counting, and my Mother Gaylynne who instilled in me to always keep God first then everything else will come. My mother raised not only her 3 biological sons but took in 3 other daughters as her own at a young age. After we were all grown, she adopted 5 more younger children. What I loved most about this was that she never treated any of us differently. These are the 3 most humble, God-fearing, giving, and selfless people I know. I can go on and on talking about them. In my eyes, they are the true meaning of (Psalms 37:25-33 NKJV) " I have never seen the righteous forsaken nor seed begging bread". Up until this point, I feel I have been living off God's Grace and their Righteousness. Now it's time for me to Create my Own.

Introduction
(My Story)

Every Relationship is either an Asset, Liability or a Lesson. Also, what we sometimes don't realize is every earthly relationship has a season. The reality is, there is no forever on earth and even the relationships we have may change depending on the season. A lot is based on what the other person or what we are going through in the season we are in. What we must do is make the best of our relationships and be the best asset that we can be. When your season is over you want your friends and family to think of the good times spent together and those memories my friend will last for an eternity. It sounds so sad but it's true. You want to be missed and had lived a fulfilled purpose-driven Life.

1. Types of Relationships

"What the Heck you got me Reading"

Romans   *12:9-10*

9 Let love be genuine. Abhor what is evil; hold fast to what is good. 10 Love one another with brotherly affection.

There are many different Relationship types. In this book, we are going to focus on only a few that are vital to your growth as a person. I hear people all of the time talking about how they don't need anybody and how they can do it on their own. WRONG. We all need each other if we want to grow and make something out of this time here on earth. The key is to find the right relationships, the positive relationships, to find the people that build you up and not the ones who break you down…

Beware of Negative Nancy. Have you ever had a person that always brings up the bad stuff and always complains about everything whether it's something personal or something in the media? This type of person may always remind you of a part of your past you no longer want to live or a not so pleasant situation in the workplace that may be close to impossible to avoid i.e. workload or scheduled breaks. The best way to deal with this person is to LIMIT YOUR INTERACTION WITH THEM!!! Show them kindness but stay FAR Away!! Complaining is contagious and all it does is prevent you from being progressive and in some cases angry about things you cannot control. Also, this will let others know that you have no control over the situation. Have you ever thought about how on social media someone can flag a picture for being offensive but something devastating or tragic stays viral forever before you can no longer find the footage? This is mind control at its best. If you are focused on the negative or injustice more than you are the solution it keeps you angry, preoccupied, and counterproductive.

Negative Nancy shows up again intentionally trying to sabotage your progress. Be very aware of these people and exposed to these negative situations. You realize these actions may be due to their upbringing. Some people become subconsciously programmed to this behavior by being around others they have interacted with all their lives. The best way to deal with them is to limit your contact and always offer positive comments and reinforcement whenever you have the opportunity.

One bad relationship can keep you from ever pushing toward your purpose and reaching your true destiny. Remember, analyze all influential relationships. This includes but is not limited to; Mothers, Fathers, Grown Kids, people you look up to, and people who you have grown up with. (note I didn't say friends because some people you grew up with don't want you to do better than them no less succeed). This may also include Coworkers, Supervisors, all other family members, people you follow, and everyone else you interact with regularly. Let's stop here. I have a few more chapters we must cover that I believe are important and extremely beneficial if you apply them to your life.

Take 2 weeks and go on a negativity fast. I want you to write down all things that don't make you feel good over the first 3 days in the log following these pages and avoid them for 2 weeks. (you have to still go to work people nice try lol.) But seriously, watch how different you feel at the end of these 2 weeks.

2-week negativity fast log

What did I find out after my negativity fast?

_____

_____

_____

_____

_____

_____

_____

_____

_____

_____

_____

_____

_____

How did my attitude change?

_____

_____

_____

_____

_____

_____

_____

_____

_____

_____

_____

How do these things make me feel?

_____

_____

_____

_____

_____

_____

_____

_____

_____

_____

_____

_____

_____

Bad relationships: can detour you from your true purpose in life. This happens more often than none. If you feel you should be an Actor or Entertainer and a family member, close friend or even Spouse instills in your head, be more realistic, watch the signs as they could be trying to sabotage your dreams. What they don't know is what you create in your head and believe in is your reality. Sometimes it gets so hard to stay focused or even push toward your dreams with all the distractions and opinions. Remember, you must do it for YOU!!! Not anybody else. At the end of the day, we go out of this world just as we came in, by ourselves. With that being said, be good to YOU! Go for It!!!

RELATIONSHIP SEASONS

2. Relationship with Self (Love Yourself First)

Ephesians 5:29 For no one ever hated his flesh, but nourishes and cherishes it, just as Christ does the church,

The First-person you encounter every day is YOU? You must learn to love yourself and have a great relationship with yourself way before you can have a healthy relationship with anybody else. Analyze who you are and what you mean to YOU. This will do wonders for your way of living. Every day when you wake up remember, I compete with nobody. I must just be a better me today than I was yesterday. I just need to show more Love today than I did yesterday. I just need to work on my goal more today than I did yesterday. I need to go a little harder in the gym today than I did yesterday. If you ate something you weren't supposed to, it's ok you just need to eat healthier today.

The thing is God doesn't make mistakes, but the beautiful part is We are allowed to.

I believe it's very important to have a relationship with God. I will go into more detail in a later chapter. The reason being, having that relationship helps you develop discernment which will help you analyze relationships you encounter. It will give you compassion for people. and the ability to show love and give love in everything you do. In Romans 12:9-10(Don't just pretend to love others. love them. Hate what is wrong. But hold tightly to what is good. Love each other with genuine affection and take delight in honoring each other.)

Create daily affirmations, Pray, and meditate. Look in the mirror and say positive things to yourself. This helps me in so many ways. This will help you start your day on a positive note. I will share a few things I say to myself every morning.

- Great Things Are Meant to Happen to Me

- My Life is Amazing

- I can Achieve Any Goal I set

- The Grace to be Wealthy is on my Life

- The Grace to Be healthy is On My Life

- God Loves Me, I Love Me"

- This is the Best Day Ever"!!!

Pretty simple Right? Doing this can change our thought process and our relationship with ourselves dramatically.

Ask yourself these questions: How do I treat myself? What am I putting in my body? (Food, drugs, alcohol) What am I doing to my body? Am I giving myself proper rest? Am I exercising my mental and physical regularly? What do I say about myself when talking about myself to others? Do I call myself fat, stupid, or Lazy? Do I say I'm smart and fit or on my way to a better me?

Seasons with Yourself

This can be a scary thought for some of us however, this is a season that is very much needed. Time with yourself helps you figure out what you want out of life and what matters most to you. The alone time I believe helps you think clearer by eliminating the noise of others. Also, it helps you get closer to your purpose through prayer and meditation and just simply allows time to think. I know life can come and, in some cases, it can come at you fast so enjoy those moments or that season of what may seem like loneliness which truly is only time for you to prepare for your next season. I wrote a song not long ago called "The Middle of the Road" and it speaks on dealing with situations within life the highs and the lows. It talks about the good and the bad. The reason I wrote this song however is to remind us to stick to "The Middle of the Road" don't let things get you down when they don't go your way. Don't let the positive moments get you so high up on the horse that it's hard to come down. Ride this wave called life and enjoy every moment of it. Keep on pushing and stay focused.

Psalm 139:14

I Praise you, For I am fearfully and wonderfully made. Wonderful are your works; my soul knows it very well.

Liability into Lesson Moment:

I used to be a liability to myself by self-sabotaging my diet knowing that I wanted to lose weight and be healthier but always letting food get the best of me. My turning point was when I looked back, and I realized I had been on this weight loss journey for over 10 years and still not getting the results I wanted. I finally looked at myself in the mirror and said if you want this to change you must Love yourself enough to change your mindset of food and change your attitude about working out. I asked myself what is the Jordan of today going to offer the Jordan of 10 years from now? Would it be a healthier me or a version of me that is borderline diabetic or have high blood pressure due to the stuff I put in my body? From that point, by the grace of God, this journey has gotten a little more productive and a little easier to handle.

What is your Liability to Lesson Moment for self? What are you currently working on in life to make yourself better for your future self? Think about that for a moment and write these things out on the next page.

(My Analysis of COMMON SENSE)

Definition of Common Sense: the sound practical judgment that is independent of specialized knowledge, training, or the like; normal native intelligence.

Your Common Sense is put together based on what is common or native to you. The two questions to ask yourself. What am I used to being subjected to? What is my story or my background? You can change your sense of common sense if you desire to. Now, this is a task that may take you a while to work on because the common sense you have has a lot to do with how you were raised and what you have subjected yourself to for long periods. I always wondered why people acted a certain way and why morally they may or may not do certain things without even blinking. Therefore, we must surround ourselves with like-minded individuals. Which is just another way of saying people who have somewhat similar common sense. If you do not do this, you will find yourself either super enlightened by the company we keep and in due time you will evolve into that level of thinking, or We can find ourselves in situations where we are extremely frustrated because common sense to you is in some cases opposite from the person you are trying to reason with. Do yourself a favor and establish those senses as soon as possible in any of your relationships that you choose. This can and will be a game-changer. You may hear people say from time to time" Sometimes Common Sense isn't so common" but that isn't necessarily the case. It is that person's common and that is why they live according to what they have been taught, they are used to, or what feels good to them for the moment. In their brain, it's either justified or it Just Makes Sense.

How is your Relationship with yourself?

_____

_____

_____

_____

_____

_____

_____

_____

_____

_____

_____

_____

_____

_____

How can this Relationship get better?

_____

_____

_____

_____

_____

_____

_____

_____

_____

_____

_____

Do I feel better about myself? If so explain.

_____

_____

_____

_____

_____

_____

_____

_____

_____

_____

_____

_____

_____

RELATIONSHIP SEASONS

3. Mentorship

"I want to Mike"   *be like*

(Philippians 4:9)

9 What you have learned and received and heard and seen in me—practice these things, and the God of peace will be with you.

Partners in Economic Progress + Mark

When I was 12 years old, I was in this program in my hometown called (PEP) Partners in Economic Progress. This was a program for young minority kids where they would give you a computer, teach you about finances, and help with tutoring as needed. One of the gifts PEP provided me was a mentor that was in the world of business. It was supposed to be someone who looked like me to encourage me that it is possible to achieve great things or "make it out the hood". In walks Mark. How did I end up with the white guy? He didn't resemble me, He didn't even live in Iowa and I couldn't see how he was going to relate to me. This has to be a mix-up! God knew! Looking back, I have to say this was a God thing and the Best mentor PEP could have partnered me with. We have been close ever since. Mark has talked me through some difficult times and has been only a phone call away. We built a lifetime relationship that has helped me through my journey throughout life. Mark went the extra mile for sure and has truly been a blessing. My mentor has a heart of gold and I pray one day I can inspire the youth in my hometown the way he helped me. I said all that to say good people are good people and a good mentor is a good mentor, it doesn't matter the person's race.

Youth Working for Positive Change

I was a part of a youth organization by the name of YWPC (Youth Working for Positive Change) under Shundrea. This group gave me my first sense of community improvement and my responsibility to my peers. We would travel and meet with other youth groups and talk about different topics that would affect us for years to come. We would plant gardens in the community and things like that. I will always remember that. We would join the peaceful demonstration. She would have us do research on governmental issues and break it down as to how it was impacting our communities. We were some teenage boys however and I know we were a hand full. Sneaking out trying to find the girls on retreats. Looking for parties But, Shundrea played no games. Get caught and you were in some serious trouble. She also made sure that we were taken care of when we took our trips. Nobody got hurt, nobody got pregnant and we always made it back home safe and sound. We had some good times together and I will never forget that.

Mr. George Shade Jr.

My Grandfather George Shade Jr. has always been my biggest inspiration/ hero and a lot of it has come from his daily walk. To be raised by someone who practices what they preach day-in-and-day-out is truly rare. I know that requires a lot of prayer and self-discipline. He raised me, and he instilled the importance of serving God and people in me. Also, the concept of being hardworking and entrepreneurship. Growing up, I was in one of two places the church or the barbershop. Thinking back, those two places shaped and instilled in me a lot of the moral values I hold dear today; like how important it is to take care of your family and those you love. My Grandfather and my Grandmother on his side. They would take us places almost every weekend growing up we were spoiled. Nobody wanted to leave grandma and grandpa's house and by the grace of God they are still like that with their Great- grandkids now.

Drill Teams

I was on the drumline in my youth and not to tut my own horn, but I was pretty good! I had a lot of mentors between the two teams, Isserettes, and the Elks drill team. Man, at the time it seemed like those guys were so hard on us, but what they did was instill self-pride, hard work, teamwork, and dedication in us. Both teams were like a brotherhood. I remember going to drill competitions and losing and wanting to cry. But way more than that I remember going and leaving with first-place trophies. We would go all over the country performing. Our team even had the honor of performing at President Obama's inauguration. I wouldn't take those experiences back for anything in the world.

Big Brothers in Business

When I was younger, I worked at a local clothing store for my friend Jermain, who is more like an older brother, called "Hip Hop Heaven" where he showed me how to run a business. He introduced me to how important it is to know your worth and how to handle day-to-day store operations and merchandising. I watched him run the store and have his kids right there with him making it happen, while still being a black man in America. Seeing all of that at the same time was extremely rare. I will always be grateful for that experience.

Rick was another business mentor, who helped me start my clothing store. This man took me to get the fixtures, introduced me to wholesalers, I mean took me under his wing! I am grateful for that. In my trucking business, I have to say my Uncle Steve and my boy Alan showed me the ropes and helped me understand the rules of this business. I took that information and ran with its people! I'm still growing and thriving in this industry today. You never know how the seed you plant in somebody can turn into a tree of reality just a few years down the line.

Bishop William Murphy III

Who, along with my grandfather, is my Pastor and a man of God that I have learned so much from. I watch and listen to his leadership week-after-week as he preaches God's word and speaks life into his flock. I watch how he sacrifices himself to do God's will, how he genuinely wants better for his people, and how he interacts with the church family. His compassion for the people never ceases to amaze me. Things such as bringing in financial advisors to teach the people, feeding also having tutoring for the families and youth every week, are the kind of selfless acts that I admire. For those reasons he's truly someone, I want to model my life after. If nothing else, I have learned from him how to be spiritual, connect with people, and how to do it all with *swag*. Truly I feel honored to be under his leadership.

Young Fyre "Super Producer"

I have watched Young Fyre from the beginning and I have been blessed to see his growth, thus far. Over the years, he has poured so many nuggets of knowledge into me. He's introduced me to the importance of meditation and how self-awareness is everything. He gives it to me straight with no chaser, even until this day. Watching how he began; I have learned that persistence and hard work does pay off.

There are many other pastors, authors, motivational speakers, people of influence, and family members that have poured into my life. I know some personally and some that I do not know, but all of whom I count as a blessing for the parts they've played in my life.

The moral of this chapter is: you may know your mentor directly, or it may be someone that has a podcast, book, or social channel where you get the information they're sharing. Either way, you're getting it, if it's bettering your life - LISTEN. I can't stress that part enough. These relationships are truly Game Changers. They can allow you to avoid a lot of hardship and mistakes in life if you just pay attention and LISTEN!

2 Timothy 2:1-2 You then, my child, be strengthened by the grace that is in Christ Jesus, 2 and what you have heard from me in the presence of many witnesses entrust to faithful men, who will be able to teach others also.

There were times in my life where people that I looked up to would tell me how I should or shouldn't do my music. Some people didn't help me excel in my music, but they wanted a piece of the results. Some people would try to discourage me from even writing this book. Some would even say you haven't lived or accomplished enough yet to write a book on relationships. Now, remember people these are some of the folks I looked up to. This is what I realized. God's Vision and what he showed me for my life is not their vision and it's not their life. Do not let people discourage you from doing what you have been purposed to do because they can't see it. Keep on pushing no matter what. If I listened to every word that people said, I may have never put out a project, a book, or spoke in public. Just because people do not think you are worthy doesn't mean that's what is true.

What are somethings that people have told you that you couldn't do that you wish you hadn't listened to? How can you change your approach? How can you get back to it? Who are some mentors or people you look up to in life? Think about that for a moment and write these things out on the next page.

Who do I see as a mentor in my life?

_____

_____

_____

_____

_____

_____

_____

_____

_____

_____

_____

_____

_____

_____

_____

Who would you like to be your mentor?

_____

_____

_____

_____

_____

_____

_____

_____

_____

_____

How can I be a mentor to someone else?

_____

_____

_____

_____

_____

_____

_____

_____

_____

_____

_____

_____

_____

_____

_____

_____

4. Friendships

"My Ride   *or Die"*

Proverbs   *13:20*

20 Whoever walks with the wise becomes wise, but the companion of fools will suffer harm.

A. Associates and Friends

Peer Pressure:

God has kept me out of harm's way more times than I have time to tell you. One instance is when I was about 19 I went out with some friends and another associate of ours Chris had beef (a problem with another person) so he was about to fight this guy who he had the beef with. The guy was friends with him. I decide to open my big mouth and tell one of the guys "if you even attempt to jump in. I'm going to knock you out" remember at the time I was 300 plus lbs. and you couldn't tell me anything. Long story short, they began fighting, and out of nowhere, I hear 2 guns shots loud. My ears begin to ring. I look back and guess what people? The guy I was talking crazy too is the one shooting in the air! We all take off running so did hundreds of other people. About 6 more shots went off that I heard but thank God nobody got shot that night. That was one of the stupidest nights of my life and to think it wasn't even my fight. I could go on and on with similar situations but let's just say God kept me. The reason I'm telling you this is because you have to be extremely cautious of the company you keep at all ages as well as being very aware of the mindset people can put you in. That could have ended my life right then and there and I wouldn't be here to write this book today. Before I left my hometown, I lost 2 friends to gun violence after just speaking to them less than 24hrs before they were killed. One less than 2 hrs. later. The fact is no one knows the time nor the place when it is time for us to meet our maker. The only thing I am saying is what you can control is the company you keep and how you move when you are around those people. Don't make yourself a target on behalf of other people's actions.

Good Friends: I have had some friends in my life that would tell me about myself even if I was wrong. Those are the friends I keep closest to my heart. Some of those people are family as well. It's such an amazing thing when people love you enough to call you on your crap no matter how it feels. If it makes you better, it's worth listening to. Nobody is perfect and once you know that and receive that for yourself you become, or you should become more receptive to positive criticism which can make you a better overall person if you take heed to the advice given.

Seasons with friends

You must see your friends in every season of their life to know if that is a true friend to you or not? How do they act when they have money? When they're broke? When you're winning? When you need them such as moving, car break down, somebody passes in your family, romantic relationship problems, etc.

You cannot hold some friends accountable for sound advice on topics that they've never encountered. I've realized some advice must be taken with a grain of salt... You don't get FINANCIAL advice from a friend that always has money problems. You don't get romantic relationship advice from a friend that can't hold a relationship down or is always cheating. You don't get parenting advice from a friend who either doesn't have kids or isn't active in their child's life. Sounds funny but these are serious things to consider. These things do not make them bad people they just aren't the ones to go to for those situations and that is what you have to analyze in each situation and relationship on a case by case basis.

I also believe that you should want to change some of your associates into friends if that relationship holds value. This is how you evolve in your circles of influence and grow your purpose. The fact remains the same if you have that friend or associate that you can only call to gossip with or go do something you don't have any business doing. You want to limit those interactions if not eliminate them eventually from your life. In those cases, you're not doing yourself or the other person any justice by continuing in that matter.

It is so important to have friends that will talk you out of making rash or stupid decisions because of emotions. Sometimes we can hype ourselves up to do something that we know we shouldn't do or in some cases, you may not know.

This type of friend is true friends and if you can keep them around for life, they will keep you grounded.

Life is all about choices. We decide in this arena of friendships, which ones we take on and which ones we don't. Don't get caught up in bringing the wrong energy into your life on your account.

Hebrews 13:7

7 Remember your leaders, those who spoke to you the word of God. Consider the outcome of their way of life and imitate their faith.

What are some situations in your life that you learned from in bad friendships? If any, what friendships should you gravitate toward or get rid of in your life now? Think about that for a moment and write these things out on the next page.

What friendships need a little a bit of fine tuning?

_____

_____

_____

_____

_____

_____

_____

_____

_____

_____

_____

_____

What Friendships do I honesty need to let go of?

_____

_____

_____

_____

_____

_____

_____

_____

_____

_____

_____

What have I done different 90 days later?

_____

_____

_____

_____

_____

_____

_____

_____

_____

_____

_____

_____

5. "The Family: Village"

Proverbs 22:6 6 Train up a child in the way he should go; even when he is old he will not depart from it.

Seasons with Family

Family Relationships can be a blessing or a burden. Let me be clear, you must Love your family but, you don't have to like them, nor do you have to allow them to bring you their burdens. Sometimes, most times; we feel like since it's family we must take on their problems or help them out when they are in a bind. I believe there is a time for that also. But that "Hardheaded Grown" family member yes, even if it is your blood child, sometimes has to learn by making and living through their own mistakes. I have seen this one too many times where the parent feels responsible for the child that turned criminal or decides to have 10 kids and put them off on Grandma and Grandpa. " That is not your responsibility. I repeat This Is NOT your responsibility! The Bible says to train a child up in the way they should go, and they will not soon depart from it. I have found this to be so true in my own life. I have made some mistakes I have got myself caught in some binds but that is on my own accord not the responsibility of the elders in my family. I had a guy tell me one-time years before I had my daughter. You will never know unconditional love until you have a child. Not only did I realize that was true in my case, but I also realized when you have that child from a toddler on up, but you're also not raising a child you are teaching principles and raising a responsible adult. No matter how cute they are. You are building someone who needs to be able to function in society.

Family: So important for dads to have a relationship with their daughters as it is important for mothers to have relationships with their sons. If either doesn't have a relationship with their child, the child doesn't know how to interact with the opposite sex as a functional adult. If you do not teach them someone else will.

Parents: I believe that if your parents took care of your obligation, you should make sure that they are taken care of when they are elderly. Remember what goes around comes around Hopefully, one day you too will make it to that elderly status, and someone will be there for you.

All other families: Help when you can but they are not your responsibility. You have one life to live and if anybody is stressing you out or taking from your quality of life Cut It Off!

Side note: be extremely careful hiring family to work for you. Some feel entitled and may take advantage, just FYI. If they are not skilled do NOT give them the job. I suggest you create one for them that they are qualified for before you sabotage your own business on their account.

Love them but sometimes personalities just don't mix and it's more heartache dealing with them than harmony. For those types of relatives, love them from a distance and help when you can.

Liability into Lesson Moment:

My Dad didn't raise me. For a long time, I would wonder why he wasn't around. As an adult, an opportunity opened where I was able to speak to both him and my mother to gain a full understanding of his abandonment. I found out there was more to it than I knew, some things were out of their control. My parents were 16 and 17 at the time that I was born. I found peace after that conversation. Nobody is perfect. This life experience taught me some unbelievably valuable lessons. One, to be the best father to my daughter that I could be by being active in her life so that she never feels some of the uneasy feelings

I felt or have similar questions during her early childhood stages. Two, to love and to understand as much as possible without holding a grudge against my dad. I've always retained the final life lesson which is to forgive. Remember, forgiveness is for yourself.

What are some situations in your family that are causing either a direct liability situation for you or an eternal battle with yourself that you need to address and turn into a lesson learned? Think about that for a moment and write these things out on the next page.

In these Relationships who are you taking responsibility for that you shouldn't?

_____

_____

_____

_____

_____

_____

_____

_____

_____

_____

_____

_____

_____

What are something you can do to change this?

_____

_____

_____

_____

_____

_____

_____

_____

_____

_____

_____

What changes did you make and how do you feel after the first 90days?

_____

_____

_____

_____

_____

_____

_____

_____

_____

_____

_____

_____

6. Romantic Relationships

"Situationships and Love" John15:12

12 "This is my commandment, that you love one another as I have loved you.

This can be the trickiest relationship of all. The reason I say this is because people can pretend to be who you need to get you to lock in with them. Not everybody is like this, but It is possible. In my life, I have experienced a few of these relationships where people are not what they pretend to be. The truth of the matter is even if they are trying to pretend the truth will eventually come out. In these relationships, if nothing else pay attention to the nonverbal signs. Is this person intrigued by certain things in which they say they are not into? Do they talk about people that are living a certain lifestyle more than they usually would talk about anything else? You are dealing with somebody that believes in the grass is greener on the other side mentality. They may never admit it to you, but they want to be just like the people that they are talking about in their regard. Do not fall victim and ignore this sign.

Seasons of the year

I had a friend tell me something and it will stick with me for life. She said " He is my Best Friend. Him being my Husband is just a bonus." That right there hit the nail right on the head for me.

The Bible talks about being equally yoked. I believe that's more than just from a religious perspective it's what you can live with what can you not handle. What do you desire for your life? Does your soulmate want the same things or similar? (i.e. do they care about credit; do they want to own a house. What are their morals, standard of living, how would they want to raise and parent your future kids if that's something that you want? Another question to ask is, where are we both really at in our seasons of life? I have personally been in two situations one where she was ready for an adult relationship and I was too young and living my best life "so I thought" and one where I was ready to put my big boy pants on and she wasn't quite ready to just chill and settle down. In both situations, I learned some extremely critical lessons in Love and respect. I learned also that no matter what you say to someone they must be ready and receptive to what you are trying to get across. Now, this principle goes across the board. Have you ever wanted so bad to prevent someone from making a mistake and you try to dictate or make them move how you want them to because you see the red flags and they still walk right into it anyway? Well, I've been the one running thru the red light and I've been the one holding the caution sign. In both, I've learned that we are all human and we have to make mistakes to grow. There is no way around it. This is where the love has to kick in and you truly figure out if this is something I can go thru with them or is this one of the conditions where I need to bow out to save myself and not compromise what I believe to be true. Nobody is better than anyone else. Some people just move a little differently and that may be ok for them but does this work for you and your life? Never get so engulfed in someone's world that you lose yourself. Never lose sight of the things that you genuinely want out of life. The things that make you happy. Life is too short to live in sadness and fear of losing a relationship.

I've mentioned two important relationships, the one with God and the other with myself. The 3rd most important relationship in my perspective is the people you communicate with daily and those who you may live with or come home to at night. This is all of the partners that we confide in and tell some of our deepest secrets and concerns. This is a person you should be able to count on for the most part. This is truly a Relationship that we choose and one that can affect our lives in the best way possible or the worst. So, let's choose wisely people.

We must be extremely careful who we allow into this position of our lives. This person must be someone that you love, can trust, and can see yourself waking up to every morning. Someone who you miss when they are away for a long period. Not someone you go to war with every other day or week.

My Grandma said something to me, and I thought to myself this is how I want to be to other people, and this is how I want my most intimate relationships to be. (All loved ones) it's simple but it means so much. She said, "you are my happiest Hello and my Saddest Goodbye" I thank God for Her and nuggets such as this.

When you think about that. It makes you put a lot in perspective when it comes to the ones you love.

In this relationship ask yourself is this someone I can build a future with. Or is this temporary and fun for the moment? If this is the case what is the timeline of that moment? I believe this relationship has a season. It may be different criteria that show what that maybe. Do we live forever? No. Have we outgrown each other or has one wore out their welcome? I believe no one should stay in a relationship if you want to grow and that person requires you to stay stagnate. Does this person allow you to be who you are? Does this person love you in the good and the bad? Does this person make you better? Do you and that person share some of the same beliefs and principles? All of these questions I'm asking you because these are the things you must ask yourself to find and realize what a healthy relationship in this area of your life looks like. It is not anybody's responsibility to make us happy. These relationships should be an additive to what you already have inside.

More times than none-people get in these Situation-ships and they settle and try to make it work. Not looking at the details of their situation because it works for the moment. We let other people pressure us on what they think is good for us. We get caught up in a certain look rather than the personality and characteristics that attract us to this person. Can this person speak your love language? Do not base your Romantic relationship based on other people's expectations or thoughts. Why? Because at the end of the day YOU must live with them.

"She's a Gold Digger she ain't looking for no broke". Y'all heard that song by Kanye. Ladies and gentlemen this is something we have to discuss.

Ladies before you expect a man to pay for this lifestyle that you want oh so dearly. Count the cost. Count the cost in how he will treat you. Count the cost in how to live that way and what you will have to go thru and sacrifice. Will this bring me a cheater? Will he be possessive, controlling, abusive, or just mean? I would highly advise ladies that you get your own money and then that man will find you. Men's Secret: a lot of guys are not looking for that IG model to wife. That is something for him to get his hands on like a new high-end car. If he is paying for everything and there is no true reciprocity in that situation-ship eventually, that man is going to get tired of cashing out or you're going to get old to him like that car and we know what happens from there. "Out with the old and in with the new" and yes having a child with him may do what they call "secure you a bag" but are you Happy? Just food for thought the next time you post a pic half-naked and pull those random dudes into your "Thirst trap" your DM. I guess it just depends on if you want something real or if you want something temporary.

Gentlemen: please take time to get yourself together before you spend your time pursuing someone when you can't even take care of yourself. This will turn into a money pit quickly and you will be mad at yourself in the end. Your women should not be taking care of you. I understand temporarily if you lose a Job or worse something to do with health. But we were created to be providers and the women were created to be our helpmeet. Work toward a purpose, secure yourself fiscally and then get that woman. Good women may seem hard to find but when you are ready God will have your Ruth in your sites. Men we have been taught more times than none getting all the ladies, being a player and chase after the one with that coke bottle shape, as being the thing to do. Yes, looks are important but they do not trump intellect and moral character, I'll tell you that much. Be careful what you pursue. Find someone with who you can be happy and build a family with. Somebody that you can see yourself having children with even if you all never have them. That's how you should search for Mrs. Right. Avoid heartache and pain by pursuing something that you know isn't any good for you. I've done it fellas I know how tempting that can be. I guarantee you will start looking at life differently if you pursue it once you get established. You're not just going to entertain just anything. Why is that? Because now this time spent is costing you something. The time spent chasing around when you're broke, and pockets look like rabbit ears was easy. But when you have something to lose the pursuit is much different.

Life is about growth, experiences, giving, and receiving love. Life to me is about finding that happy place and in this relationship find someone who can make your happy place lasts a lifetime.

What is a Romantic relationship that didn't work that you learned from?

_____

_____

_____

_____

_____

_____

_____

_____

_____

_____

_____

_____

_____

What are you experiencing currently that is a liability to your life that you need to either change or correct?

_____

_____

_____

_____

_____

_____

_____

_____

_____

_____

_____

Did you make any changes? If so How do you feel 90 days later?

_____

_____

_____

_____

_____

_____

_____

_____

_____

_____

_____

_____

7. Your Network /Business

"Network   *is Net*

worth"

Proverbs 27:17 17 Iron sharpens iron, and one man sharpens another.

Back in the day, I use to be a club and concert promoter in my hometown. Imagine, Kevin Hart and several others coming to your city to bring the best comedy show ever. I'm excited, others are excited, and when I get there only 150 people showed out. Now, this venue was huge holding up to twenty-five hundred people. Let me point out, this was not a J Shade production. Can we say lack of promotion? By the number of attendees, I'm sure you know the promoter lost a lot. It was quite embarrassing for the city yet an opportunity for me.

Did I mention I was the dopest promoter in the city at the time? I was pulled back to Kevin Hart's room where he and the other comedians were stationed, he says, I heard you promote for the biggest Hip-Hop club in the city. Of course, I say yeah that's me. They wanted to come to check it out, I said no doubt; I got you. I took them out, showed them a great time, gave them bottle service and the whole nine. At the end of the night, Kevin and his manager called me over and said, "J we appreciate you looking out for us".

The original promoter stood them up leaving me this amazing opportunity as I mentioned. I got their business cards, was told if I wanted to do another show or needed a radio drop let them know.

You will never believe what happened.... I dropped the ball. People I never called, and I lost their contact information.

This was Kevin Hart! While he wasn't the "Laugh at my Pain" or "Soul Plane" Kevin yet, he was Kevin Hart. You're probably calling me an idiot underneath your breath. That's okay. I'd be doing the same. I beat myself up for years and finally realized, this was a lesson learned.

When you have solid and direct connections you keep them and hold on to them. I vowed to never miss out on an opportunity like that again. I have since then met people all over the world and if it was a reciprocal relationship we still keep ties to this day. Never miss out on a potential blessing because of your lack of follow-up and follow-through. With this situation and a few situations before this, I was so caught up in the promoter life and being "the man". I thought that my current situation and relationships would last forever so I didn't need any new friends or business relationships. Boy oh boy was I wrong.

Life is all about networking, meeting people, and experiencing new things in life. Without doing these things you're not Living your existing and if you're going to just exist then how will you or can you ever truly step into your purpose? Finding your God-given purpose requires you to be open to what he has for you. It requires you to let your guard down and be vulnerable enough to meet new people who could be put in your path to bless you. What I have learned in business is that the most successful people in the industry want to help the ones coming up in the game. The ones that are selfish and don't want to see you win. It

means either they have some personal issues, or they are not as well off as they say. They are probably just trying to stay relevant themselves.

DISCLAIMER: Do not let people try to influence your career that hasn't had the success in the same vein that you are pursuing. Let's think about this for a minute. You wouldn't let your barber do your dental work, would you? You wouldn't let your accountant cut your hair. So why let someone who has never been successful give you advice on something that you are passionate about. I have had that happen to me too many times in my life. All it will do is leave you disappointed and discourage because you believed in somebody that thinks they know but they truly have no idea how that particular industry works, and times change.

The Bible Says in Proverbs 15:22 *Without Consultation, plans are frustrated, but with many counselors, they succeed.*

Find you a good business mentor and accountability partners that are somewhat in the same industry or the same vein as you. This move alone can be a game-changer. You are the median of the five people you hang around so find you some great people and hang on tight.

What is a Networking Liability situation you have dealt with in your life?

_____

_____

_____

_____

_____

_____

_____

_____

_____

_____

_____

_____

_____

_____

_____

How did you or can you turn this into a positive and a Lesson learned?

_____

_____

_____

_____

_____

_____

_____

_____

_____

_____

_____

_____

Did you find a mentor, or did you already have one?

_____

_____

_____

_____

_____

_____

_____

_____

_____

_____

_____

_____

8. Relationship with God

"Numeral Uno"

Matthew 6:33 But seek ye first the kingdom of God, and his righteousness, and all these things shall be added unto you

---

This is a Relationship you need to survive so you need to develop this relationship daily. A close relationship with God will help you make the best decisions in every other relationship you encounter.

You must have a relationship with a higher power "God" because this is where your true strength comes from. This is where your Joy comes from. This is who your peace comes from, in the world that we live in today. I think about how many people don't have hope for tomorrow. This is mainly because they do not believe in anything. There is no Relationship. They are just living day by day with no direction. God will give you a sense of direction. He will guide you as long as you let him in. The thing about God is, he will not force himself into a relationship with you. He wants you to want him. He wants you to fall in Love with Him. God is a God of free will and he wants to bless you and comfort you during times of storm. God will give you peace in chaos. We have to be open to this relationship, and if you are, God will be the best friend you can ever have.

In my life where I was in the wrong place at the wrong time, God still protected me. You wouldn't believe the kind of situation I put myself in more often than I want to speak of, but He kept me. It wasn't a coincidence. It wasn't luck. It was God's grace. God had bigger plans for my life, and I could have ruined what He had already purposed me to do because of being young and dumb. To be honest grown and stubborn. I know some of you all can relate to that but all in all, God kept me safe from harm and danger more times than none.

I think of different situations where a business deal fell thru, or a relationship didn't work out and I heard a voice say this isn't right you need to leave this alone or don't sign that. That was God looking out for your boy. This wasn't because I had experienced in my past, or I was an expert in this market, it was because God was watching over me and in a small voice alerted me to my spirit of discernment.

God is the only relationship that I honestly believe is unconditional because He loves us flaws and all. Matter of fact he sent his son to die for our sins because we aren't perfect. Therefore, He loves us, and He cares for us from birth until the day we die. To live a life without God in it is like riding a motorcycle at 150mph with no protective gear in the rain. Dangerous and extremely hard to see your way. I don't know about you, but I don't like how that sounds. I choose God.

Proverbs 18:24 A man of too many friends comes to ruin, but there is a friend who sticks closer than a brother.

What are somethings you can do regularly to strengthen your relationship with God? Let's come up with a game plan. A strategy to bring you closer to God. It can be reading about Him, praying, meditating, lessoning to messages, etc. Let's come up with a game plan and try sticking to it for the next 30 days. Give us some feedback on how your life has improved from this. Once again don't forget this to me is the most important relationship of all. Think about that for a moment and write these things out on the next page

What things are taking priority in my life over my relationship with God?

_____

_____

_____

_____

_____

_____

_____

_____

_____

_____

_____

_____

_____

_____

What steps do I need to take to get in tune with My Heavenly Father?

_____

_____

_____

_____

_____

_____

_____

_____

_____

_____

_____

90 Days later how has this relationship improved?

_____

_____

_____

_____

_____

_____

_____

_____

_____

_____

_____

_____

_____

_____

9. Final Words of encouragement

Thank you for taking the time out to read My book. I hope that you got something useful out of it that you can apply to your daily life. I have described different relationships and given signs and examples if they are an asset, liability, or lessons. Some can change for the better and some for the worst. What is most important is that no matter what the status. You continue to strive for greatness. Be an asset to everybody you encounter. And why is that? Cause God is Awesome and so are YOU!!!

Made in the USA
Columbia, SC
23 May 2021